*Tweets from
a Covid Cocoon*

Helen O'Rahilly

First published 2020 by
The O'Brien Press Ltd,
12 Terenure Road East, Rathgar,
Dublin 6, D06 HD27, Ireland.
Tel: +353 1 4923333; Fax: +353 1 4922777
E-mail: books@obrien.ie; website: www.obrien.ie.
Reprinted 2020
The O'Brien Press is a member of Publishing Ireland.

ISBN: 978-1-78849-253-9
Text © copyright Helen O'Rahilly
Cover illustration © Niamh Geraghty
Illustrations © Jennie O'Connell

Copyright for typesetting, layout, editing, design © The O'Brien Press Ltd

3 5 7 8 6 4 2
20 22 24 23 21

Printed and bound in Dublin by Colorman.
The paper in this book is produced
using pulp from managed forests.

Published in

DUBLIN
UNESCO
City of Literature

The Stairlift Ascends

*Tweets from
a Covid Cocoon*

Helen O'Rahilly
Illustrations by Jennie O'Connell

THE O'BRIEN PRESS
DUBLIN

Dedication

Dedicated to those who care; those who are cared for and those who have endured so much during this pandemic.

The #StairliftAscends

The #StairliftAscends started as a hashtag on Twitter back in April 2020, just a month into the first lockdown of the Covid-19 pandemic. I was then living with my ninety-year-old Aunt in North County Dublin, having returned (with my five cats) from living in London for 30 years. My life had gone from being a television executive at the BBC to being a carer for this feisty, funny woman. My mother, her sister, had died in 2019 and the Aunt was left alone in the family house. I was selling up in London and house-hunting in Dublin so we were thrown together, sharing the same home. Then Covid-19 hit in March. Due to the Aunt's advanced age and my own high-risk status (I'd survived double pneumonia in 2016), we went into our cocoon by the coast.

Already a prolific Twitter user, I put up little snippets of the daily interactions between myself and the Aunt. Some were comic, some poignant, some frustrating. Many of her finest words came as her faithful stairlift took her upstairs to bed at night: she'd send me off with her instructions for the next day or there'd be a withering comment about the day's events, or rather non-events, as nothing much was happening in lockdown. All the more reason that small interactions, a few words, a turn of phrase began to take on bigger meanings. Our chats, banter, arguments, misunderstandings show the generational differences, display the cadences and candour of her era and the impatience and frustration of mine.

The reactions I got on Twitter were instant: "She's just like my grandmother"; "God, that's my Aunt to a T'; "That's how I'm told off and I'm 55!". I'd hit a nerve with those who care for older family members: those who love them but are often frustrated by the exhausting process of daily caring. The #StairliftAscends became a favourite hashtag with a growing fan club beyond the shores of Ireland.

I would never have posted our chats to Twitter without the blessing of the Aunt Who Shall Not Be Named. "I'm 90. What do I care?" she said when asked could I publish our grumbles, gripes and giggles. "Don't put up any photos of me" was her only demand. Let me say she is the most feisty, fashion-conscious, svelte 90 year old I've ever met. Browsing the fashion rails at Arnotts or Brown Thomas, followed by a *café au lait* and a raisin Danish pastry, is her idea of heaven. She was an independent, house-owning, jet-setting woman from the 1960s onwards. A brilliant cook, she is also a gardener with an encyclopaedic knowledge of plants. I've loved her for 55 years and though she drives me mad occasionally (as I do, her), she's been a tonic during this strange, dystopian year.

We've sparred with each other, laughed, cried and survived so far. We did what we had to do in our cocoon. Even though I've moved out to live in my own home, the stairlift still ascends every night. Long may it continue to do so.

Helen O'Rahilly, Dublin

April

A month into the national lockdown. Surreal. Garda checkpoints everywhere. Rising figures of infections and deaths. Schools are shut. There's no normal Easter. "51551 - Wash Yer Hands", Joe's Liveline chant, is ringing in our ears. I was supposed to move into my new house but I'd given it to a couple of Irish medics returning from Australia who'd come back to help the national effort. Our own coastal Covid cocoon is a month old and nerves are already fraying.

Helen O'Rahilly @HelenORahilly · April 17

Aunt: Don't let that cat into my bedroom tonight.
Me: But you love her. She's been on your bed for months now.
Aunt: She looked at me funny earlier on.
Cat is asleep, oblivious, in front of fire
#StairliftAscends

Helen O'Rahilly @HelenORahilly · April 20

Me: So, tomorrow I might take you for a little spin locally so you can see the sea? Just to get you out?
Aunt: No thank you. The Gardai might stop us.
Silence

Helen O'Rahilly @HelenORahilly · April 21

Aunt: *calling loudly from sitting room* Helen, can you help me?
Me: *drops everything, rushes to front room, expecting her to have fallen*
Aunt: The cat's on my lap, could you pour me a small Jameson?
Me: ...

Helen O'Rahilly @HelenORahilly · April 21

Aunt *ascending on stairlift* Night, night!
Me: Sleep well!
Aunt: By the way, you need to do your roots: your grey is showing.
Me: Love you too!
#StairliftAscends

Helen O'Rahilly @HelenORahilly · April 22

Aunt: Helen, will you change my bed linen today?

Me: Sure.

changes bed linen

Hours later ...

#StairliftAscends

shout from above

Aunt: You put the Christmas covers on!

Me: What?

Aunt: It's April. I don't want robins and holly.

Me: *changes bed linen, again*

Helen O'Rahilly @HelenORahilly · April 22

Aunt, going to bed: You did a great job cutting the hedges today.

Me: Thanks. Yes, it was hard work.

Aunt: Tomorrow, sweep up all the stuff you cut down.

#StairliftAscends

Helen O'Rahilly @HelenORahilly · April 23

Aunt: So who was it you were chatting to on that video yoke?

Me: An old friend of mine.

Aunt: ... was it a friend or a "friend" (She makes quotation marks with her fingers)

Me: What are you getting at?

Aunt: Ah, you know ... *winks*

The day Donald Trump spoke about injecting bleach as a Covid cure.

Helen O'Rahilly @HelenORahilly · April 24

Aunt: Why is a bleach bottle on the kitchen table?
Me: I took a photo of it earlier as a joke for Twitter.
Aunt: You're not trying to poison me, are you?
Me: You'd be long gone by now if that was the case.
Aunt: While I'm at it, I've been spraying the cutlery with Dettol.
Me: *gags*

Helen O'Rahilly @HelenORahilly · April 24

Aunt: Don't bring me up tea in the morning!
Me: Ok. Why?
Aunt: I'll come down and make my own.
penny drops
Me: I. AM. NOT. TRYING. TO. POISON. YOU.
Aunt: ...
#StairliftAscends

Trump has a lot to answer for.

Helen O'Rahilly @HelenORahilly · April 25

Aunt: Will you take me for a coffee at Marks &
Spencer tomorrow? I'd love that.
Me: The café is closed for weeks now, sorry. We can't
drive beyond 2 kilometres anyway.
Aunt: *silence*
#StairliftAscends
Aunt: *under breath* You're making all this up.

Helen O'Rahilly @HelenORahilly · April 25

Aunt descends on stairlift after a nap.
Aunt: You know that fast hose you have? (Jet washer)
Me: ...yes?
Aunt: I need you to clean those three big Panda bins
with it.
Me: *sigh*

Helen O'Rahilly @HelenORahilly · April 25

Aunt: *watching Casualty* Can you do a quick vacuum for me?

Me: At 9 o'clock at night? No I won't!

Aunt: What if we have visitors?

Me: We're in a national lockdown!

Aunt: ... just in case.

Helen O'Rahilly @HelenORahilly · April 26

The Aunt's mobile phone rings in the middle of dinner.

Aunt: Hang on. I'll just go upstairs so I can talk to you.

leaves home-made dinner on table

#StairliftAscends

Helen O'Rahilly @HelenORahilly · April 26

Stairlift descends.

Me: So how was your friend?

Aunt: Same as me: miserable and stuck at home.

Me: Ah, right.

Aunt: We're both desperate to get our hair coloured and don't know how to do it.

Me: I'll do it for you.

Aunt: You wouldn't be able!

Helen O'Rahilly @HelenORahilly · April 26

Aunt: I'm exhausted. I'm off to bed.

Me: Ok. Sleep tight now.

Aunt: Goodnight Emer. #StairliftAscends

Emer is my late mother's name, her sister. I don't correct her

Helen O'Rahilly @HelenORahilly · April 27

Having watched evening news ...

Aunt: Poor Ireland. What did we do to deserve this?

Me: Deserve what?

Aunt: The virus thingy.

Me: It's GLOBAL not just Ireland.

Aunt: Oh ... I was going to say we could go to Spain to get away from it all.

Me: We can't. You can tan in your own back garden. #StairliftsAscends

Helen O'Rahilly @HelenORahilly · April 28

Me: Would you like your Jameson now?

Aunt: I spotted you had some ... Darjeeling there?

Me: *bewildered* You want tea?

Aunt: No! The present you got today!

Me: You want some of my Teeling whiskey?

Aunt: Yes, I'd like to try it.

Me: *seethes*

reluctantly pours her a small one

Helen O'Rahilly @HelenORahilly · April 29

Aunt: What am I having for dinner?

Me: Beef cannelloni, fresh salad with toasted pine nuts and a fresh herb dressing.

Aunt: ...

Me: What?

Aunt: I can't do that 'winding pasta around the fork' yoke.

Me: You just cut this pasta.

Aunt: Would have preferred pork chops.

Me: ...

Helen O'Rahilly @HelenORahilly · April 29

I'd made a tomato and garlic ragu sauce from some stunning North County Dublin tomatoes that a kind, farmer neighbour had left at our front door.

Me: So did you like the cannelloni?

Aunt: I did but ...

Me: What?

Aunt: It was too ... tomatoey.

Helen O'Rahilly @HelenORahilly · April 29

Aunt: I'm off to bed.

Me: Sleep well.

Aunt: Sure what's the point in getting up tomorrow?

Me: To feed the cats?

Aunt: They're your cats, you do it.

Me: Thanks.

Aunt: You should have left them in London.

Me: ...

#StairliftAscends

Helen O'Rahilly @HelenORahilly · April 30

#Stairlift Ascends

A shout from upstairs ...

Aunt: Helen, there's two of your cats on my bed!

Me: Which ones?

Aunt: The black and white one and Low-Low (it's "Lola" but she calls her after her low fat spread.)

Me: Do you want me to move them?

Aunt: ... ah sure, no. It's a cold night. (She has an electric blanket.)

Helen O'Rahilly @HelenORahilly · April 30

Aunt: Is that thing they were talking about on the telly tonight?

Me: What thing?

Aunt: The yoke that caused a fuss on the radio with Joe Duffy.

Me: Oh, the teenagers in love? "Normal People" it's called.

Aunt: Is it on?

Me: Next week. Tuesday night. Why?

Aunt: I want to see what all the fuss is about …

She watched one episode and was, quote, "bored stiff" within ten minutes.

May

The lockdown is extended to May 18. We get a 'national roadmap' but it still feels like a bit of a cul de sac. I drive the Aunt to my new house to sort out the garden: a lockdown project that takes our minds off the tedium of four walls and those 6pm updates on the figures of loss and infection. I begin to spend the odd night in my house. Aunt is not pleased.

Helen O'Rahilly @HelenORahilly · May 1

Aunt: Night. I'll be up at 7AM.

Me: You're always up at 7AM.

Aunt: ... for you to do my hair colour.

Me: Well, I will *not* be up at 7AM to do your hair colour!

Aunt: ...

Me: 11AM will suit me, after a coffee.

Aunt: *silence*

#StairliftAscends

Helen O'Rahilly @HelenORahilly · May 2

Aunt: Night, night.

Me: Sleep well now.

Aunt: I'm happy with my hair.

Me: Great to know!

Aunt: The next time, don't try and drown me.

Me: Right, so.

#StairliftAscends

Helen O'Rahilly @HelenORahilly · May 3

Aunt: I hear it's a Bank Holiday tomorrow.

Me: It is.

Aunt: I hate them.

Me: I know.

Aunt: Everyone goes out and your mother and I never went anywhere.

Me: So you've told me.

Aunt: Awful.

Me: Well, nobody is going anywhere now.

Aunt: Oh yes. Good!

#StairliftAscends

Helen O'Rahilly @HelenORahilly · May 4

Aunt: I had a nice day today.

Me: Good.

Aunt: We sorted your new garden, didn't we?

Me: Well ... you shouted instructions at me.

Aunt: Well?

Me: Nothing. You had some good advice.

Aunt: Can we go back tomorrow?

Me: ...

Aunt: if it's sunny I'll bring my suntan lotion.

Helen O'Rahilly @HelenORahilly · May 6

Aunt: You never did what you said you'd do today.

Me: *puzzled, could be anything* What did I not do?

Aunt: The big Panda bins. Wash them out!

Me: *sigh* I'll get to it.

Aunt: It's been weeks now.

Me: Are you keeping a diary?

Aunt: Yes.

Me: ...

#StairliftAscends

Helen O'Rahilly @HelenORahilly · May 7

Aunt: Have you put out the bins?

Me: Yes.

Aunt: Did you wash them?

Me: How can I wash them when they're full of rubbish?

Aunt: We'll get a reputation for having dirty bins.

Me: A reputation?

Aunt: People talk ...

#StairliftAscends

Helen O'Rahilly @HelenORahilly · May 10

Aunt, heading to bed: I'd like the tabby one tonight.

Me: Pardon?

Aunt: The cat. Low-Low.

Me: Lola.

Aunt: Him.

Me: Her.

Aunt: Well, let her in to my room.

Me: It doesn't work like that with cats.

Aunt: It's worked so far.

#StairliftAscends

Helen O'Rahilly @HelenORahilly · May 11

Aunt: Have you locked the back door?

Me: Yes

Aunt: The front door?

Me: Not yet. I leave it open in case Cookie (neighbour's cat) needs to be let out.

Aunt: He rules this house.

Me: *neither a ginger cat or I rule this house*

Aunt: He's a bit of a git.

#StairliftAscends

Helen O'Rahilly @HelenORahilly · May 13

Aunt: You see those cracks in the fence posts?

Me: *squints* Barely. What about them?

Aunt: Can you fill them in with concrete?

Me: Concrete? We don't have any.

Aunt: Well, get some.

Me: The DIY shops are closed!

Aunt: Polyfilla, then?

Me: ...

Helen O'Rahilly @HelenORahilly · May 14

Having procured some concrete from a neighbour ...
Aunt: You did a good job on the fence posts today.
Me: Oh good. Glad you like them.
Aunt: Pity it's a different colour.
Me: That's because the new concrete is drying out.
Aunt: Otherwise you'll have to repaint them all tomorrow.
#StairliftAscends

Helen O'Rahilly @HelenORahilly · May 15

Aunt: I'd love a cup of tea.
Me: I'll put the kettle on.
Aunt: You know, you have so many followers on Twitter ...
Me: And?
Aunt: I don't know ... how come you're still single?
Me: ...

Helen O'Rahilly @HelenORahilly · May 15

After a bit of a spat on Twitter with a troll …
Aunt: *heading to bed* Don't be feeling sorry for yourself now just because some nasty person doesn't like you.
Me: I'm not! I've got thousands of lovely followers.
Aunt: … but don't be getting a big head either, now.
#StairliftAscends

Helen O'Rahilly @HelenORahilly · May 18

I go to pour a nip of whiskey. Bottle empty.
Me: Did you pour your own whiskey tonight?
Aunt: I did.
Me: There's nothing left for me.
Aunt: Sure you can get some more tomorrow.
Me: *silently fumes*
#StairliftAscends

Helen O'Rahilly @HelenORahilly · May 20

Aunt: Before you go tomorrow, will you vacuum the stairs?

Me: I'll be off very early (heading to my house).

Aunt: Well the stairs are full of cat hairs.

Me: *squints* I can't see any.

Aunt: *Your* cats' hairs.

#StairliftAscends

Helen O'Rahilly @HelenORahilly · May 22

Phone call to Aunt after her many, failed attempts to find Virgin One on telly.

Me: Turn it off and back on. *six minutes of silence*

Aunt: I've now got RTÉ One.

Me: Leave it there, forget about Virgin. You can watch the Late Late …

Aunt: No. I'd rather go to bed.

#StairliftAscends

Helen O'Rahilly @HelenORahilly · May 27

Aunt: What time are you bringing me to the garden centre?

Me: 11ish?

Aunt: I'll be up at 7AM.

Me: I won't.

Aunt: I don't know how you held down a job for so long at the BBC.

Me: … we'll go at 10AM so …

Aunt: That's better.

#StairliftAscends

Helen O'Rahilly @HelenORahilly · May 31

Aunt: The TV is broken.

Me: It isn't. You used the wrong remote.

Aunt: And that pie you left me was awful.

Me: Did you cook it in the oven?

Aunt: No, in the microwave.

Me: It's oven-cook only.

Aunt: ... and the stairlift is not working.

Me: I fixed it.

Aunt: We'll see, later ...

Helen O'Rahilly @HelenORahilly · May 31

Later ...

Aunt: Are you sure this (the stairlift) is fixed?

Me: It is.

Aunt: You didn't fiddle with the electrics, did you?

Me: No! I can't and wouldn't do that. It was just a stuck cable. I sorted it.

Aunt: Maybe you should call the engineer anyway?

Me: I FIXED IT. IT WORKS.

Aunt: ...

#StairliftAscends

Me: Told you.

June

Chief Medical Officer Dr. Tony Holohan becomes a National Treasure. We hang on his every word. "Phase 2 Plus" begins on June 8. Department stores will start to reopen: this brings joy to the Aunt, who's been pining for a browse in Arnotts. Even though I'm spending more time at my house, the cats remain with the Aunt and, naturally, become bargaining chips.

Helen O'Rahilly @HelenORahilly · June 4

Phone call at night.

Aunt: I can't find Benjy.

Me: Who is Benjy?

Aunt: Your cat.

Me: His name is Dougie.

Aunt: She's missing.

Me: It's a *HE*. Look on the kitchen chair.

Aunt: Oh ... there she is.

Me: He. He. He.

Aunt: She's grand. Night, night.

Helen O'Rahilly @HelenORahilly · June 5

Aunt: It's a bit late for you.

Me: For what?

Aunt: For you to be driving to your new house.

Me: I'm staying *here* with you tonight.

Aunt: That makes a change.

Me: *sigh* I've been living here with you 24/7 for nearly 9 months now.

Aunt: But you'll be going tomorrow?

Me: I will.

Aunt: See? Told you.

Helen O'Rahilly @HelenORahilly · June 8

Aunt: People are going back into town again!

Me: Well some places are open again.

Aunt: Arnotts?

Me: No.

Aunt: Brown Thomas?

Me: No.

Aunt: Penneys?

Me: Sorry, no.

Aunt: Where are they all going then? Sure what's the point then?

Department stores reopen tomorrow for the first time since lockdown.

Helen O'Rahilly @HelenORahilly · June 9

Aunt: We're going to Arnotts tomorrow?
Me: No way! It will be jammed.
Aunt: Well, bring me to get my hair done then.
Me: Hairdressers don't open until the end of June.
Aunt: WHAT? *under her breath* This is the worst year of my life.
She is 90

The changing rooms are off limits so she'll have to risk buying off the peg.

Helen O'Rahilly @HelenORahilly · June 10

Took Aunt, masked, to Dunnes Stores.
Aunt: I'm delighted with my new jeans and shirt.
Me: *driving us home* Oh good.
Home, 20 minutes later
Aunt: *shout from upstairs* The jeans are too big and the shirt is too small. We have to go back now!
Me: *sigh*

Helen O'Rahilly @HelenORahilly · June 11

Made an appointment to bring the Aunt to socially distanced shopping in Arnotts.
Aunt: This is so good. I've been waiting since February!
Me: You can have a good browse now.
Aunt: ... but ...
Me: What?
Aunt: There's no way I can go ...
Me: I'm driving you!
Aunt: ... with my hair in this state!
Me: *sigh*

Helen O'Rahilly @HelenORahilly · June 11

Me: I'll be staying at my own house tomorrow night. Your recycling bins will be washed by Panda on Saturday morning so leave them out on the street when they've been emptied tomorrow.
Aunt: *under breath* Always away when something needs to be done.

Helen O'Rahilly @HelenORahilly · June 13

Fixing the Aunt's dishwasher.
Me: *making pained, guttural noises while wearing soaked jeans and half-buried in a kitchen cupboard*
Aunt: Can you do this without getting water on the floor, please?
Me: *screams a silent profanity*

Helen O'Rahilly @HelenORahilly · June 15

Arnotts outing with Aunt.
Aunt: First, my make-up.
Me: Brand?
Aunt: It's French.
Me: Estée Lauder?
Aunt: No.
Me: Dior?
Aunt: No.
Me: Clinique?
Aunt: No.
Me: Chanel?
Aunt: There it is! *walks off*
Charlotte Tilbury, British

Helen O'Rahilly @HelenORahilly · June 15

Aunt browses the fashion rails. I go to the lingerie department.
Aunt: What did you get?
Me: A few pairs of Sloggi knickers.
Aunt: Oh. I'm surprised they do them in your size.
Me: ...

Helen O'Rahilly @HelenORahilly · June 15

Now in Marks & Spencer.
Me: I got you some nice things to eat in the Food Hall. Did you spot anything to wear?
Aunt: Ah, no. Sure it's all for aul wans.
Me: ...

Helen O'Rahilly @HelenORahilly · June 15

Back at the Aunt's house, post shopping trip.
Aunt: *pokes at my bag* What's in there?
Me: New bras. I usually get new ones every few months.
Aunt: Black. Black. Black.
Me: So?
Aunt: Try pink or beige. Much more flattering.

Helen O'Rahilly @HelenORahilly · June 18

Phone call.
Aunt: Are you coming home?
Me: I AM home, my home.
Aunt: I mean home, *here*.
Me: Why?
Aunt: Someone's in your bed.
Me: WHAT?
Aunt: ... a big lump in your bed.
Me: *sigh* It's my duvet cover, wrapped up.
Aunt: Ah. No wonder it wouldn't answer me.
Me: ...

Helen O'Rahilly @HelenORahilly · June 18

Aunt: I hope you're around in the morning. There's a lot of things that need to be done here.
Me: I have my own house to worry about now. What sort of things are so urgent?
Aunt: We need Fairy Liquid.
Me: Is that it?
Aunt: I could do with an apple tart. Not from Tesco.
Me: ...

Helen O'Rahilly @HelenORahilly · June 22

Aunt on phone: I have a date to get my hair done next week!

Me: Brilliant! Did M (her hair stylist) ring you?

Aunt: Yes! Well as a long-term customer I'd expect that but it was very nice of her to call me.

Me: All glam again! (I asked M to call the Aunt)

Aunt: Pity you hadn't called her, like I asked you to do.

Me: ...

Helen O'Rahilly @HelenORahilly · June 22

Aunt: You'd want to book yourself in for a good cut.

Me: I'm quite enjoying the longer look so I'll wait a bit.

Aunt: ...

Me: What?

Aunt: You're a bit ...

Me: WHAT?

Aunt: ... dishevelled looking.

Me: Thanks.

Aunt: You're welcome.

Helen O'Rahilly @HelenORahilly · June 27

Stairlift descends.

Aunt: I forgot my water.

Me: I would have brought some up.

Aunt: Sure I'm down now.

Me: My Twitter pals tell me T.K. Maxx is open tomorrow.

Aunt: I'll be ready at 9AM.

Me: *sigh* Can we make it 11AM?

Aunt: *sighs* Well, I suppose. You're the driver.

#Stairlift Ascends

Helen O'Rahilly @HelenORahilly · June 29

On the first morning that hairdressers re-opened I have a trim.

Aunt: Mother of God!

Me: What?

Aunt: Where's your hair gone?

Me: I had it cut this morning.

Aunt: But ... but ... it's all gone. You're like one of those ... boot boys.

Me: Ah now. The top still has length.

Aunt: Well, I'm glad your mother isn't alive to see this.

July

The airports are almost empty. People are taking holidays at home. We feel we're in a bit of a Covid reprieve as the nightly toll is dropping. I take a respite break in the West. Creamy pints with food only but so very welcome. The Aunt has help at home but I keep the phone on 24/7, just in case. She doesn't disappoint ...

Helen O'Rahilly @HelenORahilly · July 7

Day 6 of my Connemara holiday.

Aunt on phone: Benjy (cat) looked at me and he was really angry.

Me: His name is Dougie. How did you know he was angry?

Aunt: He looked angry.

Me: Did he scratch you?

Aunt: No.

Me: He was probably just looking for a cat treat.

Aunt: You need to come home now. They're going feral.

Helen O'Rahilly @HelenORahilly · July 10

Still on holiday in Connemara.

Aunt on phone: I thought you were coming back today?

Me: No. I was always due back tomorrow.

Aunt: The stairlift isn't working. Nor the TV and I can't work the oven.

Me: They all work. Read the instructions I wrote out for you.

Aunt: My glasses are not good.

Me: I will be back tomorrow.

Aunt: Not today?

Helen O'Rahilly @HelenORahilly · July 11

Back from holiday.

Aunt: So it all fell apart when you were away.

Me: What did?

Aunt: Everything.

Me: And that's my fault?

Aunt: …

Me: The stairlift, the telly, the plants that died in the garden? My fault?

Aunt: Well, you weren't here.

Me: …

Helen O'Rahilly @HelenORahilly · July 11

Aunt: I don't like this whiskey.

Me: Sorry about that.

Aunt: It's not Jameson.

Me: No, it's Connemara, a peated whiskey.

Aunt: Well I don't want the taste of a turf briquette in my mouth.

Me: I thought you might like a change?

Aunt: No. I don't. No.

Helen O'Rahilly @HelenORahilly · July 12

Aunt: So I need new plants to replace the ones that died when you were away.

Me: Your garden is gorgeous. It's packed with plants.

Aunt: So, take me to Tully's Garden Centre tomorrow.

Me: Not to Mass?

Aunt: You have to book for that. No. Garden Centre please.

Me: ...

Helen O'Rahilly @HelenORahilly · July 17

Aunt on phone: Two of your cats are still here.

Me: You wanted to keep one.

Aunt: Do I?

Me: Yes. I'm picking Lola up tomorrow.

Aunt: But I love Lola.

Me: You told me she vomits hairballs on the carpets.

Aunt: She does. I'll cope.

Me: I'll take Minnie then.

Aunt: But I love her too …

Helen O'Rahilly @HelenORahilly · July 20

Aunt: I'm running out of food to feed your cats.

Me: What? I bought new boxes on Friday. How many packets are left?

Aunt: *disappears from phone for SEVEN minutes*

Aunt: 13 packets.

Me: *sigh* They won't starve tonight.

Aunt: They are pigs.

Helen O'Rahilly @HelenORahilly · July 29

Aunt: You took my two cats.

Me: *My* cats. Sorry. I was worried about you bending down to feed them.

Aunt: But now I miss them.

Me: I'll bring you to see them in my house.

Aunt: It's not the same.

Me: No more hairballs, panic poos, no hair on the couches.

Aunt: ... you made the right decision.

August

*Now living full time in my own place and clicking
on my Covid Tracker every day. The cats are safely
ensconced in my house. Without me and the cats,
the Aunt is kept happy with trips out: Dundrum Town
Centre, The Pavilions, Grafton Street. It's like Christmas
has come early for her.*

Helen O'Rahilly @HelenORahilly · August 3

Aunt on phone: Are you taking me out this week?
Me: Well I got a tip about a lovely garden in Wicklow
where we can wander and have a coffee.
Aunt: Can I shop there?
Me: Eh ... no: it's a garden with a café.
Aunt: Is Arnotts not open?
Me: ...

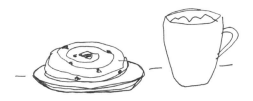

Helen O'Rahilly @HelenORahilly · August 10

Aunt on phone: A load of Marks & Spencer dinners appeared in my fridge.

Me: I know. I got them for you.

Aunt: How did they get there?

Me: I put them there this morning!

Aunt: Were you here this morning?

Me: Yes.

Aunt: I notice there's no Chicken Balti. I love those.

Me: ...

Helen O'Rahilly @HelenORahilly · August 12

Phone call to Aunt.

Me: Would you like to go out to Sunday lunch up the coast this weekend?

Aunt: Where?

Me: A lovely place, does fresh seafood. Has great reviews and has a view out to the sea.

Aunt: Ah no. Sure I have the beach here beside me.

Me: ...

Helen O'Rahilly @HelenORahilly · August 14

Drive to my Aunt's house to get her pension.

Me: Your PPS card is not where it usually is.

Aunt: It's always there!

Me: Not now.

40 minutes of chaos ensues

No card. I drive home. Phone rings.

Aunt: Found it! It was in the black handbag.

Me: I searched that bag!

Aunt: No. My *other* black handbag.

Me: ...

Helen O'Rahilly @HelenORahilly · August 16

Lunch out.

Me: So, have whatever you like: there's lovely fresh seafood. Have a main and a dessert or a starter and a dessert or all three!

Aunt: ...

Me: What?

Aunt: I ate a Danish pastry before we came out. I'm not hungry.

Me: You forgot I was taking you out to lunch?

Aunt: Yes.

Me: ...

Aunt: I'll just watch.

Helen O'Rahilly @HelenORahilly · August 19

Aunt on phone: I hear Storm Helen is coming tonight.

Me: Ellen. Storm Ellen.

Aunt: Oh, that's odd.

Me: What is?

Aunt: She's been in trouble.

Me: Who?

Aunt: Ellen.

Me: *penny drops* DeGeneres?

Aunt: Bullying at her show, so I heard. Why would they name a storm after her, so?

Me: ...

Helen O'Rahilly @HelenORahilly · August 30

Shopping trip to Grafton Street.

Me: So, after a coffee in Bewleys, we'll go to COS to have a look at clothes?

Aunt: *spots Bewleys* There's a huge queue.

Me: So? I've been longing for an almond bun since February.

Aunt: Well I'm not waiting. Marks & Spencer's Café will do.

Me: But ...

Aunt: M&S! I am not queuing for a bun I could make at home.

sets off in direction of M&S

Helen O'Rahilly @HelenORahilly · August 30

In COS, Wicklow Street.

Aunt: That's nice. *points at dress*

Me: Do you want to try it on?

Aunt: I meant for you.

Me: You know I don't wear dresses.

Aunt: ... about time you started, you might find someone.

Me: ...

Helen O'Rahilly @HelenORahilly · August 30

Car is parked right outside the Stephen's Green Centre. We're walking back slowly to it.

Me: *carrying two heavy bags of shopping in one hand, Aunt hanging off my other arm*

Aunt: *lets out huge sigh*

Me: What's up?

Aunt: Oh it's all too much. I'm never doing this again.

Me: ...

Helen O'Rahilly @HelenORahilly · August 30

In car, en route home to Aunt's house.

Me: So, did you enjoy town?

Aunt: ... I didn't buy anything.

Me: Well we got some food that you love and I got some clothes.

Aunt: Jeans and a black shirt? Sure that's not fashion. You've hundreds of those. You're very stuck in your ways.

Me: ...

September

Videos of house parties and the odd raucous pub scene cause national consternation. We stick to masked-up shopping trips. The most excitement we get is bagging rare flu shots in advance. Level 3 restrictions come in, mid-month. Here we go again ...

Helen O'Rahilly @HelenORahilly · September 3

Phone call.

Aunt: So what are the weekend plans?

Me: I'm out at a supper tomorrow.

Aunt: ...

Me: ... and on Saturday I'm having an old college pal over for dinner here.

Aunt: I meant me.

Me: What?

Aunt: What are you doing with me?

Me: ...

Helen O'Rahilly @HelenORahilly · September 6

8AM phone call.

Aunt: Is Kildare Village open yet?

Me: (semi-comatose) What?

Aunt: I want to go to Kildare Village.

Me: I think I have to reserve a parking space before we can go.

Aunt: Well can you do that? For this week? There's sure to be a sale on.

Me: ...

Helen O'Rahilly @HelenORahilly · September 6

Shopping with Aunt in mall.

Me: There's a nice design on this jumper.

Aunt: *fiddles to find label* Acrylic! Never!

Me: What about this one?

Aunt: Polyester mix. No.

Me: Ok. This one's 100% cashmere.

Aunt: How much?

Me: €69.99

Aunt: Are you MAD?

Me: ...

Helen O'Rahilly @HelenORahilly · September 7

Supermarket shopping with Aunt.
Me: *checks her list* So you need apple tart, fresh custard, brown bread, milk, fresh soups, 7-Up, vegetables and whiskey?
Aunt: Yes.
Me: *buys all the above*
arrives at Aunt's house and opens fridge
Me: You've already got an apple tart, fresh custard, milk, soups, 7-Up and vegetables!
Aunt: Yes but we got some whiskey.
Me: ...

Helen O'Rahilly @HelenORahilly · September 13

Phone call from Aunt (post Kildare Village day out).

Aunt: You should have bought that jacket.

Me: Which one?

Aunt: The one in ... Rich ... Riss ...

Me: Reiss?

Aunt: The blue one.

Me: It was a size 12. If I was 18 years old it would have fit me.

Aunt: ... we could let out the seams?

Me: ...

Helen O'Rahilly @HelenORahilly · September 15

Late night phone call.

Aunt: I didn't see you today.

Me: No, I was out for a walk.

Aunt: Where?

Me: The Hill of Tara.

Aunt: Sure that's not far from me.

Me: I was having my own day off today, as I told you on Sunday.

Aunt: But you were only a few miles away.

Me: I'll see you tomorrow.

Aunt: But you were so close ...

Helen O'Rahilly @HelenORahilly · September 18

New Level 3 restrictions come in for Dublin. The phone rings.

Aunt: I suppose I won't see you until November now.

Me: Why?

Aunt: Dublin is shut down.

Me: I *am* in Dublin.

Aunt: But you're miles away.

Me: 25 minutes away!

Aunt: You should never have moved.

Me: (I'm glad I did) I'll see you Sunday.

Aunt: Don't infect me now!

Helen O'Rahilly @HelenORahilly · September 21

Phone call.

Aunt: I didn't see you today.

Me: You saw me yesterday.

Aunt: Where were you today?

Me: I was out for a walk on Dollymount Strand.

Aunt: Sure you were there as a child.

Me: I haven't been there for 40 years.

Aunt: But sure it's still the same!

Me: ...

Helen O'Rahilly @HelenORahilly · September 22

Phone call to Aunt.

Me: So we have appointments for our flu shots on October 6th: you at 11.30AM, me at 11AM.

Aunt: ... mmmm

Me: Also we're both getting our bloods done at your house at 8AM on the 8th. We have to fast, so no Barry's tea at 7AM!

Aunt: You're trying to kill me.

Me: ...

Helen O'Rahilly @HelenORahilly · September 23

Phone call at 7.30AM.

Me: mmmmhello ...

Aunt: I just got an urgent demand in the post. From Panda.

Me: What?

Aunt: URGENT so it is!

Me: I was ASLEEP!

Aunt: It says the gas meter needs reading!

Me: That is not urgent. I was fast asleep!

Aunt: Well you better come up and sort it out.

puts down phone

Helen O'Rahilly @HelenORahilly · September 30

Aunt on phone: Any chance of bringing me to
Arnotts?

Me: Well, now is not a good time with the virus
spreading and the tougher restrictions. What is it that
you need from there?

Aunt: Black tights.

Me: Sure I can get you black tights anywhere.

Aunt: *audible sigh* But it's the *going out* I like.

October

Level 5 lockdown hits the country mid-month. I get to know the Gardai on Operation Fanacht as I whizz between home and Aunt. I offer them sweets. Level 5 is an 'end of the world' scenario for herself: wartime words pepper her speech. To be fair, she did live through that 'Emergency'.

Helen O'Rahilly @HelenORahilly · October 4

Birthday girl Aunt phones: I loved the jumper, thanks very much.

Me: Did you have a nice day?

Aunt: I did.

Me: All those cards, flowers, presents.

Aunt: ...

Me: Was there something you didn't like?

Aunt: Ah ... no ... well ... I didn't get a single sweet.

Me: ...

Helen O'Rahilly @HelenORahilly · October 6

I phone the Aunt.

Me: Are you ok?

Aunt: I suppose ...

Me: You saw X today and Y looked in on you?

Aunt: ... yes.

Me: You still have your 100 Euro in your purse?

Aunt: ... yes.

Me: So you're grand?

Aunt: I could have done with a trip to Arnotts.

Me: ...

Helen O'Rahilly @HelenORahilly · October 12

Phone call.

Aunt: I liked that basmati curry yoke you got me.

Me: Oh good. I had a fresh Dosa tonight.

Aunt: A dose of what?

Me: A *D.O.S.A* – a crispy, savoury Indian pancake. With coconut chutney and vegetable curry.

Aunt: ... sounds lovely.

Me: You eat it all with your hands.

Aunt: ... ah now!

Helen O'Rahilly @HelenORahilly · October 12

Aunts phones to remind me that the gas fire in her sitting room is still not working.

Me: I've told you that the engineer is very busy but he's coming on Wednesday. I'll be there to deal with him.

Aunt: Ten days now, sitting in the kitchen ...

Me: With a TV and two hot radiators! You're not freezing.

Aunt. No ... but I miss looking out the front window. I keep an eye on the street, you know ...

Helen O'Rahilly @HelenORahilly · October 13

My phone goes off at 5am.
Man: This is the Care Network Alarm System. Are you the next of kin for Ms …
ME: YES!
Man: Her alarm has been activated.
Me: *rings Aunt in panic* ARE YOU OK? YOU SET OFF YOUR WRIST ALARM!
Aunt: I'm in bed. I'm grand. I just put my Ruth Rendell down on it.
Me: …

Helen O'Rahilly @HelenORahilly · October 14

Aunt has picked up that the lockdown level might get even higher.
Aunt phones: You won't be able to see me now!
Me: Calm down. I will.
Aunt: Dublin is a prison!
Me: As your carer I can travel to look after you.
Aunt: But you'll be stopped by the Gardai at the checkpoints!
Me: They let me through.
Aunt: Are you bribing them?
Me: …

Helen O'Rahilly @HelenORahilly · October 15

Me: I missed a call from you. Are you alright?

Aunt: I ran out of 7-Up. Have you any?

Me: It's 9 o'clock at night! I'd need to drive up the motorway to you. Is it for your whiskey?

Aunt: Yes.

Me: Have it with some water?

Aunt: Oh god no, it'd taste of whiskey then.

Me: ...

Helen O'Rahilly @HelenORahilly · October 16

Me: Isn't it worrying about old Fungie all the same?

Aunt: Who?

Me: The Dingle Dolphin! He's gone missing.

Aunt: Sure he's only a fish*.

Me: Fungie is a national institution!

Aunt: He had a good innings. We all have to die sometime.

Me: ...

*mammal, I know

Helen O'Rahilly @HelenORahilly · October 17

I phone the Aunt.

Me: I'll be on Radio One about my college days tomorrow.

Aunt: Oh god, no!

Me: What do you mean?

Aunt: The neighbours!

Me: What about them?

Aunt: You're not talking about sex or drugs are you?

Me: *takes deep breath* At 9 o'clock in the morning on RTÉ?

Aunt: I know you ...

Helen O'Rahilly @HelenORahilly · October 18

I phone the Aunt after the radio programme is broadcast.

Me: You didn't ring me. What did you think?

Aunt: About what?

Me: My piece on Sunday Miscellany this morning?

Aunt: What?

Me: *sigh* You missed it, didn't you?

Aunt: Can you ring me tomorrow? I'm in the middle of watching a good detective yoke on the telly.

Me: ...

Helen O'Rahilly @HelenORahilly · October 19

Visit to the Aunt (Part 1)
(After a stressful morning, I eventually get to her house with the weekly shop)
Aunt: What kept you?
Me: My car was broken into. The battery was drained. I had to get the AA out. Then go and get a new battery and only then could I do your shopping.
Aunt: But I didn't get my Danish pastry for my elevenses.
Me: ...

Helen O'Rahilly @HelenORahilly · October 19

Visit to the Aunt (Part 2)
Me: So, would you like to hear my bit on Sunday Miscellany from yesterday?
Aunt: What's it about?
Me: My college days.
Aunt: Sure I know about those. I have you here, I don't need to hear you talking about yourself.
Me: ...

Level 5 lockdown comes in at midnight

Helen O'Rahilly @HelenORahilly · October 21

Aunt: Can you come up to me? It's urgent!

Me: What's wrong? Have you had a fall?

Aunt: No. There's a load of leaves in the front garden. You need to sweep them up.

Me: *sigh* I don't think that is "essential" travel, to be honest.

Aunt: Well it's essential to me!

Helen O'Rahilly @HelenORahilly · October 23

Aunt: My lights have dimmed, what do I do?

Me: Your electric lights or do you think you're dying?

Aunt: NO! My ceiling lights are flickering. Do I shove my stick into the fusebox?

Me: DO NO SUCH THING! Get your carer to ask next door if they have the same issue.

Aunt: ... I usually just give it a bash with my walking stick.

Me: ...

Helen O'Rahilly @HelenORahilly · October 29

Aunt: I don't believe all the shops are shut. I'm going into town on the bus tomorrow.
Me: You are NOT! The Gardai will stop you and you'll get a criminal record.
Aunt: I don't care.
Me: They will stop your Saorview TV service. No more "Judge Judy".
Aunt: ... oh.
Me: (*result!!*)

Helen O'Rahilly @HelenORahilly · October 29

Aunt: There's nothing for me to eat!
Me: I brought you five Marks & Spencer dinners today! Look in the lower shelf of your fridge.
Aunt: *sounds of rummaging*
Me: All your favourite things!
Aunt: ... but you didn't put them on my favourite shelf!
Me: ...

Helen O'Rahilly @HelenORahilly · October 31

Aunt: Are you coming up tomorrow to plant those
bulbs in my garden?
Me: *sigh* Yes, I am.
Aunt: Can you go to the supermarket for me first?
I have a list.
reads out long list
Me: *pours whiskey*
Aunt: Did you get all that?
Me: I did. (I didn't.)

Helen O'Rahilly @HelenORahilly · October 31

Halloween evening.

Aunt: It's like The Blitz here!

Me: You didn't live in wartime Britain so how would you know?

Aunt: Well, I have an imagination!

Me: So, houses destroyed, bodies all over the place, fire brigades putting out huge fires?

Aunt: ... always with the smart remarks.

November

We wade through the treacle of life under Level 5.
I cheer her up by telling her I'm writing this book for
Christmas but she adds that she'll have to go "into
hiding". I tell her she's already there.

Helen O'Rahilly @HelenORahilly · November 1

At the Aunt's after doing the shopping.

Me: So, you owe me ... €49 for the two shops I did for you.

Aunt: *mutters under her breath*

Me: What?

Aunt: You're FLEECING me!

Me: WHAT? You have the till receipts in your hands. You ASKED me to buy these things.

Aunt: *Silently counts out 49 Euro coins*

Me: ...

Helen O'Rahilly @HelenORahilly · November 2

Late night phone call.

Aunt: The washing machine has flooded the kitchen!

Me: Why on earth did you put it on at this hour?

Aunt: I was distracted earlier in the day.

Me: By what?

Aunt: YOU!

Me: So ... it's MY fault that the kitchen is flooded?

Aunt: And now I've had to put down my Sunday newspaper to soak up the flood ...

Me: ...

Helen O'Rahilly @HelenORahilly · November 3

Me: You know the little stories I put up on Twitter about you and me?

Aunt: You're being sued?

Me: NO! I'm thinking of publishing a booklet of them for Christmas.

Aunt: Sure who'd want to read our old guff?

Me: If it sells well, Arnotts will be your oyster.

Aunt: Fire ahead!